Women and Economy: The Politics of Empowerment

Bushra Zulfiqar

Women and Economy: The Politics of Empowerment

LAP LAMBERT Academic Publishing

Impressum/Imprint (nur für Deutschland/ only for Germany)
Bibliografische Information der Deutschen Nationalbibliothek: Die Deutsche Nationalbibliothek verzeichnet diese Publikation in der Deutschen Nationalbibliografie; detaillierte bibliografische Daten sind im Internet über http://dnb.d-nb.de abrufbar.

Alle in diesem Buch genannten Marken und Produktnamen unterliegen warenzeichen-, marken- oder patentrechtlichem Schutz bzw. sind Warenzeichen oder eingetragene Warenzeichen der jeweiligen Inhaber. Die Wiedergabe von Marken, Produktnamen, Gebrauchsnamen, Handelsnamen, Warenbezeichnungen u.s.w. in diesem Werk berechtigt auch ohne besondere Kennzeichnung nicht zu der Annahme, dass solche Namen im Sinne der Warenzeichen- und Markenschutzgesetzgebung als frei zu betrachten wären und daher von jedermann benutzt werden dürften.

Coverbild: www.ingimage.com

Verlag: LAP LAMBERT Academic Publishing AG & Co. KG
Dudweiler Landstr. 99, 66123 Saarbrücken, Deutschland
Telefon +49 681 3720-310, Telefax +49 681 3720-3109
Email: info@lap-publishing.com

Herstellung in Deutschland:
Schaltungsdienst Lange o.H.G., Berlin
Books on Demand GmbH, Norderstedt
Reha GmbH, Saarbrücken
Amazon Distribution GmbH, Leipzig
ISBN: 978-3-8383-8887-8

Imprint (only for USA, GB)
Bibliographic information published by the Deutsche Nationalbibliothek: The Deutsche Nationalbibliothek lists this publication in the Deutsche Nationalbibliografie; detailed bibliographic data are available in the Internet at http://dnb.d-nb.de.

Any brand names and product names mentioned in this book are subject to trademark, brand or patent protection and are trademarks or registered trademarks of their respective holders. The use of brand names, product names, common names, trade names, product descriptions etc. even without a particular marking in this works is in no way to be construed to mean that such names may be regarded as unrestricted in respect of trademark and brand protection legislation and could thus be used by anyone.

Cover image: www.ingimage.com

Publisher: LAP LAMBERT Academic Publishing AG & Co. KG
Dudweiler Landstr. 99, 66123 Saarbrücken, Germany
Phone +49 681 3720-310, Fax +49 681 3720-3109
Email: info@lap-publishing.com

Printed in the U.S.A.
Printed in the U.K. by (see last page)
ISBN: 978-3-8383-8887-8

Copyright © 2010 by the author and LAP LAMBERT Academic Publishing AG & Co. KG and licensors
All rights reserved. Saarbrücken 2010

Women & Economy: The Politics of Empowerment

By: Bushra Zulfiqar

Dedicated to my father who taught me to live, love & let go

Table of Contents

Chapter 1: Introduction 6
    1.1 Introduction 6
    1.2 Context 7
    1.3. The Question 8
    1.4. Introducing the Core Concepts 8
    1.5. Research Methodology 8
    1.6. Study Structure 9

Chapter 2: Literature Review 10
    2.1. Roadmap 10
    2.2. Women Empowerment- The Conceptual stream 11
        2.2.1. Historical Evolution 11
        2.2.2. Understanding women empowerment 12
        2.2.3. Measuring empowerment-the critique of measures 14
    2.3. Women's Economic Participation & Empowerment: The Contested Linkage 15
    2.4. The Conceptual Framework 19

Chapter 3: The Research & Argument 21
    3.1. Pakistan: Land of the Pure 21
    3.2. Women in Pakistan 22
    3.3. The Research 22
        3.3.1. Objectives 22
        3.3.2. Methodology 23
        3.3.3 Limitations 23

3.4. Qualitative Data Analysis	23
3.4.1. Rawalpindi City-A Profile	23
3.4.2. Format of Semi-Structured Interviews	24
3.4.3. Women & their Views	24
3.5 Data Analysis	35
3.5.1 Key Argument	35
3.5.2 Main Findings	35
Chapter 4: Conclusion	39
References	42

Acknowledgements

I wish to place on record my gratitude for my two incredibly inspiring professors Dr. Silvia Posocco and Dr. Sylvia Chant who very skilfully transferred into me a tiny bit of their passion for improving the status and condition of women in today's world. It is this personal quest that they have excited and a sense of academic curiosity which forms the basis of this piece of work. Thanks are also due to my supervisor Dr. David Lewis for his continued guidance throughout the journey.

CHAPTER 1: INTRODUCTION

1.1. Introduction

The last two decades have witnessed an increasing emphasis on women's empowerment as gender has moved at the centre of all development debates and interventions. International commitments like the Millennium Development Goals (MDGs) and the Convention on the Elimination of all forms of Discrimination against Women (CEDAW) have brought women's empowerment as an extremely important component of all development interventions across the globe. Women's empowerment has been approached with a variety of rationales such as women's empowerment through improved access to educational opportunities, women's empowerment through participation in the political process and provision of economic opportunities including but not limited to micro-credit programmes. I have been intrigued by the market or economic participation approach towards women's empowerment. I always found the linkage very logically constructed. It was only during my Gender, Globalization and Development course at the London School of Economics that I discovered the kinds of injustices and inequalities working women, particularly from the third world are subjected to. A deeper and closer look at the lives and experiences of these women revealed a different story, which raises a lot of questions about this conventional linkage. I felt that the first hand story of these working women was under told. This desire of helping the voices of these women heard by development policy makers, researchers and parishioners is the key motivation behind this research. Its spirit lies in understanding the different conceptualizations and manifestations of empowerment from the perspective of women. As I started reading around the subject, I began feeling that perhaps the first step towards women empowerment should be to let them decide the kind of power or empowerment they want for themselves. I felt that without a truthful and real understanding of women's perspective on empowerment, based on sound objective research and data, it is not possible to have meaningful policies for improving the status of women. Therefore this study is an in-depth investigation of the concept of empowerment and it's relationship with economic participation in the personal lives and struggles of grass root women. Women empowerment has to be promoted on the basis of an understanding of women's lives as understood and defined by themselves. However, in doing so, the study does not look at women as passive or inferior victims of discrimination but aims to learn from their impressions and experiences to inform policy, practise and discourse on women's empowerment.

1.2. Context

The geographical focus of my research is my own country Pakistan. Women's empowerment has been a major theme in Pakistan's national development policies ever since the inception of the country. The Constitution of Pakistan guarantees non-discrimination against women and advocates full participation of women in all spheres of national life. Successive governments, both military and democratic have tried to elevate the socio-economic status of women through various policy approaches adopted in their respective terms. Today, although the status of women in Pakistan varies across economic, social, rural/urban and religious/ethnic divides, gender inequality remains high and intense in every sector of public as well as private life. Domestic violence, gender discrimination in access to education, health care facilities and career opportunities are to mention but a few of the manifestations of the social subjugation of women in the society. Policy failure, lack of commitment and political dis-continuity along with a seriously constrained resource and institutional base contribute to this situation. The disconnection of research and academic debate with policy and practise in Pakistan has further exacerbated the problem. I hope that this investigation becomes a meaningful contribution in the limited primary research available on Pakistani women. This book is being documented at a time when the Government of Pakistan is in the process of formulating its National Policy for Women. I hope this research has policy relevance and in some way it helps the Government improve the fate and reduce the fallings of Pakistani women.

1.3. The Question

The objective is to explore the link between women's economic participation and empowerment, based on women's own view points. . I want to understand whether women themselves see empowerment primarily in terms of economic participation and its resulting benefits. In addition to the literature, I will also try to draw on the first hand experiences of women, from a small sample. Therefore question I will seek to answer is:

How far does an approach to women's empowerment that links it with economic participation reflect grassroots womens' own perceptions and experiences?'

1.4. Introducing the Concepts

There are two core concepts here. The first one is women's economic participation and the second one is women empowerment. For the purpose of this research, I would like to briefly define both of them in the introductory section.

1. **Women's economic participation:** A host of factors like age, education, occupation, marital status, family structure, household dynamics and power structure have a strong bearing on women's economic activity. However, for the purpose of this study economic participation includes any activity with monetary compensation which could be paid employment or waged labour (Kabeer, 2008)

2. **Empowerment:** I will intentionally not define empowerment because the purpose of my research is to conceptually understand empowerment from the perspective of women and arrive at an understanding of this seemingly abstract concept, and also find out it's relation

with their economic participation. What follows from here will itself lead not only to the definition but also a deeper understanding of this concept, defined by women themselves.

1.5. Research Methodology

This study is based on both primary and secondary research. I will start with a critical analysis of the existing literatures on women participation in the economic sphere and their empowerment. I will analyze both the conceptual as well as the policy debates, particularly in relation to my research question. I will then move on to presenting my primary research where I interacted with women in the field to understand and document their understanding and experiences of empowerment (details in chapter 3). The views of women about their experiences of empowerment and economic participation will be the central in the findings of this research. Finally an effort would be made to ascertain the policy relevance along with the conclusion.

1.6. Study Structure

The introductory chapter lays out the objectives and justification for this research and defines it's scope. Chapter 2 synthesizes a critical review of the current conceptual debates on women's empowerment and traces the historical evolution of the concept. In the same chapter, I will also discuss the conceptual framework deduced from the literature reviewed which forms the basis of my primary research. In the third chapter, I present an analysis of the research findings from the field. Last but not the least chapter 4 summarises and concludes the research along with drawing policy implications and identifying areas for further research.

CHAPTER 2: LITERATURE REVIEW

2.1 Roadmap

In this chapter, I have basically tried to summarize and critically analyze the academic debates and existing body of literature on the subject of women's empowerment. I have to say that an extremely vast body of diverse kinds of literature including the conceptual, theoretical, research and policy related debates on women's empowerment exist. However, given the time constraint, I have focused on the literature of the past two decades. The following diagram depicts the range of thematic literature areas I have reviewed and will subsequently refer to in my research.

Figure 2.1 Thematically Overlapping & Inter-linked areas reviewed to study Women's Empowerment

I will try to deconstruct the concept of women's empowerment and capture it's multiple dimensions from different gender and development approaches. A range of both the conceptual and policy related debates have been dedicated to economic empowerment of women but the focus on grass root women's perspectives, experiences and expectations has been very little. Where there has been primary research, women's own voices have not been predominant in the discourse generated, particularly in Pakistan which is the geographical focus of my research.

As I started reviewing literature on this subject, I realized that a lot of meaningful research and theoretical insights about women empowerment exist but fall short of being translated into concrete policy decisions and then their on ground implementation. Gender equality has all the complexities of a social and cultural process of change which has enormous challenges when it comes to policy responses. From a social policy perspective, women's empowerment is an area which represents the real world development challenges and on ground realities which make effective policy implementation the challenge that it is.

2.2. Women Empowerment-The Conceptual Stream

A lot has been researched and written about women empowerment. It is one of the most widely used terms in development literature and it is incorporated as a cross cutting theme in development goals of poverty alleviation, livelihood security, social inclusion and sustainable development. I would try to analyze through the literature review is whether how deep the research or literature has gone in conceptualizing and deconstructing the term 'empowerment', and explore it's cause and effect relationship with economic participation.

2.2.1 Historical Evolution

Women empowerment has so far been addressed under the two major frameworks: (i) women in development (WID) and (ii) gender in development (GAD). While the former emphasizes the participation and inclusion of women in existing development processes, the later came as response to the limitations of focusing on women in isolation. GAD recognizes gender as a social relationship between men and women which has subjugated women and has consistently kept them at a position of disadvantage. It highlights the importance of involving and targeting men to address the gendered constructs of masculinity and feminity (Moser: 2005). Ever since then, the objectives of achieving gender equality, women empowerment and elimination of all kinds of discrimination against women have been framed, revisited and revived in various international conferences such as the first World Conference on Women held in 1975 in the city of Mexico. It has been followed by three major subsequent conferences in 1980, 1985 and 1990 to revisit and re-affirm the commitment to achieve gender equality and women empowerment (Taborga: 2009). The year 2000, witnessed the Millennium Development Goals (MDGs) which were endorsed by the world community from the platform of the United Nations. The third of these MDGs is exclusively related to women empowerment i.e. **to promote gender equality and empower women.** Although progress has been made in some of the indentified indicators, a lot more needs to be done in all sectors and sub-sectors if gender equality and women empowerment is to be achieved in due time.

In the literature, there is a growing realization that women empowerment is a complex processes with deeply embedded social and cultural constructs, which define the scope and limitations of this empowerment. Conceptually women empowerment is often equated with being able to make choices in life. Given this linkage, it implies that women who are economically engaged are able to make choices for themselves. In reality the exercise of choice is restricted by a range of factors and gendered perceptions of masculinity and feminity which obstacles gender equality or an improved status for women (Kabeer: 1999).

2.2.2 Understanding Women Empowerment

Despite a considerable degree of realization of empowerment being a complex process, there has been little if no effort to deconstruct the concept of empowerment and use it as a tool to address the underlying issues gender inequalities as noted by Kabeer, one of the contemporary writers on women empowerment. She has divided women empowerment into three main components: (i) agency, (ii) resources and (iii) achievement (Kabeer: 2005) and argues that their inter-play and inter-relationship with each other can have positive outcomes for empowerment. An effective and transformative agency which challenges the gender biased notions, improved recognition of women's role in the household work and their say in policies and decision making can enhance the status of women. However, her definition does not build in the patriarchal mindset of both men and at times women who accept and scum to gendered discrimination defined by socio-cultural norms and traditions.

On the other hand, Betata in 2006 has argued that empowerment is not an outcome but a process which has elements enabling or restricting it. She has divided empowerment into issues of personal autonomy, control over body and sexuality and religiosity which are predominant in the private sphere of womens' lives and fall beyond the tangibly defined aspects of empowerment. She has also gone a step forward to recommend a new indicator of women empowerment which is **Gender Empowerment Enabling Environment (GEEE).** The GEEE pinpoints towards the legal as well as cultural dimensions and societal attitudes required for enabling the empowerment of women in relation to men.

There is also a considerable debate about the vocabulary of women empowerment. Part of the conceptual stream argues that gender empowerment is a wrong choice of term. Gender refers to the socio-cultural constructs about the roles and responsibilities of men and women and gender empowerment may mean strengthening the existing differential and discriminatory practices between the two. However, in very few articles I found the term gender empowerment replaced by women empowerment. Perhaps, another gap in the existing literature is the lip service like recognition of the mention of men's role in uplifting the status of women. There is little if no academic writing exclusively on policies and strategies of involving men in the process.

There is also very little effort to distinguish the levels of empowerment i.e. individual, household, community or society? The dynamics of levels and different stages of empowerment at these levels has to be made a permanent part of the discussions and discourse on women empowerment. Empowerment is a very relative concept which cannot be defined universally. No one, man or woman can achieve absolute empowerment, rather people experience different dynamics of empowerment at different stages of their lives. (Mosedale: 2005).

2.2.3. Measuring Empowerment-the Critique of Measures

In addition to the conceptual abstraction of the term empowerment, the literature also identifies problems when it comes to measuring empowerment. Previously different interventions by governments, donors or NGOs had women empowerment as their shared objective but mostly without having a well defined method or indicator of measuring it. It was in the mid 90s that the United Nations Development Programme (UNDP) developed the Gender-related Development Index (GDI) and Gender Empowerment Measure GEM). The GDI into life expectancy, education and earned income whereas the GEM comprises of proportion of seats held by women in national parliaments, percentage of women in economic decision making positions and the female share of income (Beteta 2006). Both of these indicators have been severely criticized for being gender blind. Beteta in her work has argued that these measures do not deal with relative inequality between men and women, build up on international data bases rather than data from national governments and exclude the real gender based power relations.

There has also been a fundamental negligence of non-economic and invisible aspects of empowerment in these indicators, for example having a say in usage of contraception and issues relating to marriage, child birth and fertility. Similarly, I find the measures of participation in economic or political spheres fairly limiting in scope as participation may be controlled or dictated and therefore not very meaningful. The whole politics of participation include the decision of who participates in decision making and who doesn't is not really taken into account by these indices. The shortcoming, particularly in relation to my topic is that it does not include the deeply embedded underpinnings of gender identities, constructs and inequalities which are at times re-enforced by the women's economic participation and are vital in measurement of empowerment. It does not recognize that the distribution of household work as unnatural and socially defined. It does not flag the inter-household power relations underpinning the labour division. The triple role of women including child birth and raring, domestic household chores and communal responsibilities do not get recognized by the GEM. Elite-class female politicians who get elected to parliament -with backing of influential figures are not representative of actual state and realities of the majority of women, in the rural and the grass root levels, particularly in the developing countries. These indicators have been extensively criticized for measuring gender inequality amongst the educated and economically better off women and ignoring other non-economic aspects of empowerment.

2.3. Women's Economic Participation & Empowerment: The Contested Linkage

Throughout the 70s, 80s and 90s, the levels of women's economic participation have grown all over the world. However, the trends of female labour force participation or their participation in the informal economy have been uneven and varied. Stichter in 1990 has noted that in virtually all societies, men have higher labour force participation rates than women but there are incredibly varied inter-societal differences in female labour force participation due to gendered cultural practices. Female labour force participation whether through paid employment, waged labour or in informal economy remains a highly problematized and contested sphere.

Women's economic participation has traditionally been a controversial theme, it's statistics have been criticized for being gender blind as women's work go un and under reported. It is due to the fact that women's household responsibilities and care work which includes but is not limited to cooking, washing, cleaning, fetching water and fuel, looking after the livestock and cattle, tending to the sick and the elderly (in extended household structures) is virtually neglected by all measurements of labour force participation and GDP (Kabeer: 2007). The domestic work of women is not reported in the census or other data collection methods partly because it is not considered as work which needs to be compensated and partly because it gets effected by gender biased survey and data collection methodologies where women are virtually neglected.

Clearly related to the topic of women economic empowerment is the whole paradigm **of micro-credit and loans**. While many believe women to be less creative entrepreneurs than men and less reliable for the repayment of loans, in reality the situation is quite the opposite. Many independent evaluations have found out women to be much more reliable clients than men; they are better investors with quicker and higher rates of repayment. Goetz and Gupta (1996) in their analysis of Grameen Bank and three other credit institutions in Bangladesh has indicated that only 37 per cent of the female borrowers retain control over their loans within the household. This means that in 63 per cent of the households where women have taken a loan in their own name, men have partly or completely used the money for their own priorities. Nonetheless, a woman who takes a loan remains responsible for repayment by the bank, even when her husband uses the loan without generating any return on investment. Ultimately, some women may even be worse off with a loan than without it. Even in the literature on women's economic empowerment, there is little if no recognition of the non-economic gender based roles, responsibilities and subjectivities having a direct bearing on economic empowerment. Empowerment has to be understood <u>holistically</u> and <u>relatively</u> i.e. in relation to men, in relation to different women groups and at different levels.

However, for the working women in most of the developing countries, the nature of work and it's social dynamics does not shift the balance of power in their favour. It does not improve their status in relation to men. If one is to imply that economic participation leads to empowerment, then one can argue that a CEO of a company is a highly empowered person, but empowerment has a strong non-economic dimension and a very rich person may not necessarily be empowered. I would like to argue here that authority cannot guarantee empowerment, neither can participation. They are highly relative concepts which have different meanings and interpretations for individuals and a generalized 'one size fit all policy' cannot be applied upon all. Women's participation in economy can lead to a reduction in incidents of domestic violence or can enhance their access to information and mobility but at the same time, it can also mean the exploitation of their labour by men who assert complete control over women's earnings. There have been numerous examples in all parts of the world, where men have inflicted physical, mental or psychological violence over women for getting hold of their income or not allowing them a say in where their money is spent. Even the kinds of exploitation women are subjected to at workplace are many. Low and differential wage rates, long working hours, tough working conditions, health and environmental risks and sexual harassment are some of the many manifestations of such of female labour exploitation. This scenario makes the linkage between economic participation and empowerment very complex and superfluous. To me, the most important issue in the empowerment discourse is the women's own vision and views about empowerment, which is what I will try to find throughout this research

As I was reviewing the literature, I figured the striking linkage between poverty and women empowerment. It is mostly the poor women, who become the worst victims of dis-empowerment in a complex environment of gender inequality. The term **feminization of poverty** reflects the helplessness of women and seems to quite clearly explain the obstacles in women's empowerment. Their vulnerability to discrimination and exploitation becomes very high, in both explicit and implicit ways. For example, men have a major contribution in formal economy; have regular contracts, high income and more leisure time than women. Also, men tend to spend a higher share of their income on personal expenditure whereas a major chunk of women's earnings are spent in the household expenditure and consumption items, in the interest of family members. (Staveren: 2001). Women do get adversely effected by the international financial policies since cuts are imposed in non-formal sectors and women workers mostly confined to the lower informal ends of the economy suffer. Women undertake multiple economic activities, both in public and private domains most of which remain invisible. The terms feminization of work seems to converge with the informalization of work undertaken by women (Kabeer: 2008). In times of crises, the amount of both paid and un-paid manual work that women do increases with no distribution of care work and household responsibilities with men. There are scenarios where even un-employed men do not lend a helping hand to women due to the traditionally defined norms of masculinity (Staveren: 2001). It becomes extremely important to target men for undoing a mindset which is built on gendered identities and a stubborn gendered association of roles and responsibilities.

However, all is not gloom. Women's participation in formal economy has considerably improved and changes are occurring in the gendered division of labour. This is due to a wide range of factors like education, rural-urban as well as international migration, demographic changes, declining fertility and family size, globalization and technological advancement, though the pace of change is slow. The push factors towards female participation in formal economy have been many including commertalization of agriculture sectors, landlessness, recession and increased cost of living and lack of state provided social and health care services (Kabeer: 2008). Also the phenomenon of globalization which I feel has tremendously transformed the way both men and women experience their lives. The increased economic and social restructuring of the world has had a strong bearing on gendered subjectivities, roles and responsibilities. It has in many tilted the balance of power on the women side by offering them a wide range of economic opportunities even in professions which were traditionally considered male dominated e.g. pilots, scientists, economists and politicians. Factors like access to information and independent media have catalyzed a process of social change around the world which has tampered with deeply embedded gendered identities to quite an extent. I think one can safely that the changing social and economic inter dependence between states has sharply highlighted the role of women in both public and private spheres and enhanced their status to an extent but the issue is that relative inequality. Gender equality and women empowerment have to make men and women equal partners with equal powers. It is for this complex relativity that women empowerment discourse has to be informed by an on-going analysis of poverty and gender in –equality and in-equity.

However as a student of gender, I find the happy acceptance of oppression and gendered discrimination by women most worrisome. Gender to date has been a deeply problematic areas mainly because it is unquestioned and unchallenged by women themselves. I would like to confess that my intention of making women realize this unnatural and unjust division of roles has manifested into the basis of my dissertation, which focuses on the experiences of grass root women's perceptions. It is an indirect effort to make them realize that the gendered injustices and inequalities they live with are socially determined and can be questioned.

2.4. The Conceptual Framework

It was not possible to summarize all the literature I reviewed in the space available though on the basis of all the literature reviewed particularly in relation to my research, the following conceptual framework was constructed.

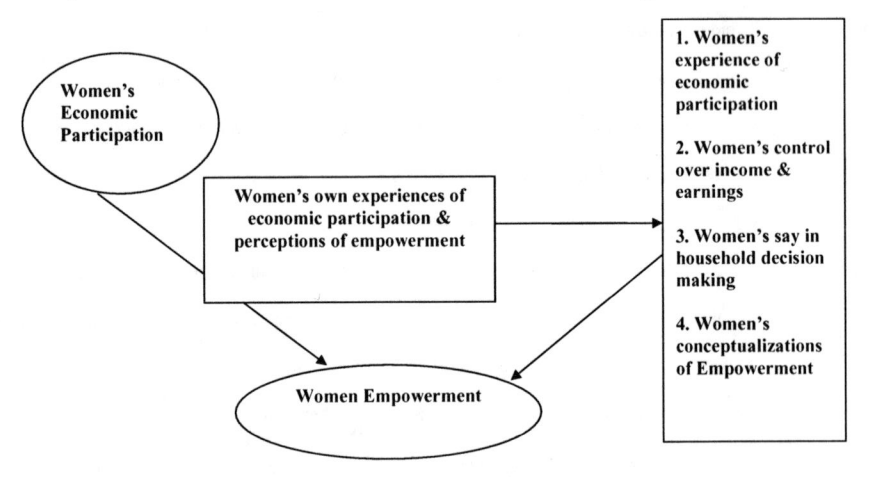

Figure 2.2   Deconstructing Women Empowerment: The Conceptual Framework

Keeping women empowerment at the centre of analysis, I will try to track it's relation with their economic participation based upon women's own experiences and views on both. As mentioned earlier, the research objective is to understand empowerment from the lens of grassroots women. Based on the literature reviewed, I have developed four broad determinants of empowerment, to be able to collect information from respondents and acquire an understanding of the power relations in their life domains. They are (i) women's experience of economic participation, (ii) women's control over income and earnings, (iii) women's say in household decision making and (iv) women's conceptualizations of empowerment. However, these determinants of empowerment do not in any way pose a limit to the women's vision of the concept but are useful in initiating the debate and discussion with the women in field.

CHAPTER 3: THE RESEARCH & ARGUMENT

3.1. Pakistan: Land of the Pure

Pakistan is located in South Asia at the cross roads of Central Asia and the Middle East. It is bordered by Afghanistan and Iran in the west, India in the east and China in the northeast. Pakistan is a federation of four provinces (Punjab, Sindh, NWFP & Balochistan), federally administered tribal areas (FATA), federally administered northern areas (FANA) and the Azad Jammu Kashmir (AJK). According to the United Nations figures, the estimated population of the country in 2009 is 180, 800, 000 making it the sixth most populous country in the world. About 20% of the population lives below the international poverty line whereas around 43% of the population is under the age of 15. About 52% population is male and 48% female, the male/female ratio is 108: 100 and average household size is 6.8.

Pakistan is linguistically a diverse country where more than six languages are spoken though Urdu is the national and English is official language for communication. In sixty two years of it's life, the country has been through different phases of democratic and military rule and has seen stints of acute political instability. Economically, the basis of the country has been shifted from mainly agricultural to a strong service base. Agriculture now accounts for only 20% of the GDP and the service sector for about 53%. There has been significant progress in the field of education and through rigorous educational reforms introduced, the Government expects to achieve 100% enrolment amongst children of the primary age group and 86% adult literacy rate by 2015.

Pakistan has been through an interesting process of social change and has seen the emergence of a strong middle class in the last few decades. The traditionally extended and hierarchical family structure is rapidly shifting to urban, smaller and nuclear households because of high rural-urban migration in search for economic prosperity and social uplift.

3.2. Women in Pakistan

'While growing up in South Asia is a perpetual struggle, to be a woman in this region is to be a non-person. Women bear the greatest burden of human deprivation in South Asia.' - Mahbub ul Haq

An average Pakistani woman lives a life in a vicious circle of oppression, injustice and inequality of opportunity. Women in Pakistan are stigmatized the inferior status assigned to them by the patriarchal basis of the social fabric and gender based discrimination between men and women in every sphere of public and private life. Women remain confined to the four walls of the house which is defined as it's ideological and physical legitimate space. Whereas men are predominant in the public sphere, ruling the world outside the home. This demarcation of roles and responsibilities flow from a strong culture of patriarchal institutionalized in the institution of purdah (veil). The gendered social processes and behaviours have intensified the commodification of women who are seen as mere commodities representing the honour of the men. The tradition of purdah is an extension of this ideologue. Patriarchy has manifested itself in multiple forms like son preference, provision of educational opportunities to male child at the cost of the girl and socio-cultural restraints upon acquiring skills and accessing the market. It is due to the still unanswered questions of women's consistent subjugation and suppression in Pakistan that I wanted to find out how would the women feel empowered about their lives.

3.2 The Research

3.2.1. Objectives

As mentioned earlier, this dissertation builds up on first hand experiences of women about participation in economy and views about empowerment. It required field work which was carried in Pakistan during March and April of 2009. The research had the following multiple objectives:-

1. **To hear from women's about their personal experiences of economic participation**
2. **To find out if their economic participation had led to their empowerment**

3.2.2. Methodology

Due to the time constraint, I could only focus on only one city within Pakistan. Therefore the city I chose was that of Rawalpindi which also happens to be hometown. The research tools I used were **semi-structured interviews** and **participatory observation** as it was the requirement of the study. The focus of my research was about personalized experiences of women which could not be gathered by close ended survey questions so in order to encourage the women open up to me, I had to interview them in informal semi-structured one to one discussions. I chose a small sample size of six working women representative of different age groups, occupation and marital status through **purposive sampling** whereas my unit of analysis was the **household**.

3.2.3. Limitations of the Study

1. It was difficult to get the women answer the question exactly
2. Some of the respondents did not open up very much which would have held back a lot of information

3. Time constraint limited the study to women of one city only and the findings cannot not be generalized on women all over Pakistan
4. I could not expand the small sample size because the information and discussion generated from more would have occupied more space than allocated for data in the dissertation

3.3. The Qualitative Data

3.3.1. Rawalpindi City-A Profile

Rawalpindi is a city located in the Punjab province of Pakistan, near the capital of Islamabad. The city's covered area is about 154 square kilometres and according to the Government's estimate has a population of 3,039,550 people. It's literacy rate is 70.5%. The population is ethnically and linguistically diverse as the city has a high influx of immigrants coming from the rural areas of Pakistan primarily in search for employment. Rawalpindi is considered as an economic hub of Pakistan which is host to numerous industries and factories, large scale businesses, medium and small scale enterprises.

The reason I chose Rawalpindi was it is my home town and being a woman from here, I wanted to better understand the experiences of economic participation and empowerment of other women of my city. Also, the time and logistical constraints did not allow a further geographical expansion of the study.

3.3.2. Format of Semi-Structured Interviews

The respondents were encouraged to talk in the following order

1. Respondent to tell about herself
2. Respondent to talk about her experience of economic participation
3. Respondent to talk about why, where and how she spends her salary and who retained control over her earned money

4. Respondent to talk about her participation and say in the family's decision making and the power relations within the household
5. Respondent to talk about her concept of empowerment, whether she considers herself empowered

3.3.3. Women & their Views

Respondent no 1

Profile:

Name: Zareen Bibi

Age: Approximately 42 (approximately)

Marital Status: Married with 5 children

Occupation/Nature of Work: Factory worker/ paid employment

Household Structure: Nuclear

Excerpts from semi-structured interview

1. 'I got married at a **very young age** (how young, I can't exactly remember) but my **children were born very soon** after my marriage. My husband was a cab driver then. His salary was very low and we were just too many. It was very difficult for him to feed us all so I also started looking for work. The children were very young, one was just an infant and I would always worry for him but then what other choice did we have. I used to work on a day to day basis till my neighbour took me to this garment factory where she used to work before her marriage. Now it has been ten or twelve years that I have been working there.'

2. 'I don't find my work difficult, now I am quite used to it. It is **fine and delicate** thread work which needs concentration and hard work but if you want to earn money, you will have to work hard wherever you go. I work out of necessity, if my husband's income was enough

for us, I would have preferred to stay home. This would have allowed my **eldest daughter** to attend school or learn some sewing skills because now she is the one who stays home and cooks for everyone. This has comforted me in some ways because when she was also too young, I had to work in the factory till evening and then **come back and cook**.'

3. 'My salary is very little. We are poor people who hardly make both ends meet. There is nothing left to be saved. The good thing is that I do manage the kitchen expenditure all by myself. I feel happy that me and my children are not just parasites on my husband's income but I contribute even in weddings of our relatives. Though it is little that I do but I try not to go empty handed, I don't like that.'

4. 'It has been ages that I have stopped thinking about myself, it is my children about whom I think and wish well for their future. My husband is not a bad man, after all he has kept me and my children for the last seventeen or eighteen years. **Decision making is solely his domain and I think it is best to keep it that way.** He takes **correct decisions** and owns them. The only time he gets angry is when he comes home from work and the dinner is not ready. Even then he doesn't beat the children, sometimes in his anger he starts throwing utensils at me. **Of course I don't like that but what can I say**. I cannot beat him back but I do shout back sometimes. But it is okay, it is normal.'

5. 'I don't know what do you mean by empowerment but in my view I cannot keep working for a very long time now. I have spent all youthful years of life working but I am old now and I do feel very tired. But if I stop working, the future of my children will get effected. I have to save money for the **dowry and marriage of my daughters**. They have grown up fast and in a few years would be ready for marriage. A mother wants the best for her daughters, even if she

is poor. I will be happy if my daughters get married off in good families. I don't want anything for myself.'

Researcher's Observations

This respondent was not in good health, she constantly coughed and breathed heavily. The house had two semi-cemented rooms with one room exclusive for her husband and the second one for the respondent and her five children. Her two girls were busy cleaning the house whereas the boys were playing around barefoot in dirty clothes. The picture was that of poor family struggling to make both ends meet.

Respondent no 2

Profile:

Name: Maria Shah

Age: 25

Martial Status: Single

Occupation/Nature of work: School Teacher/formal economy

Household Structure: Nuclear

Excerpts from semi-structured interview

1. 'I teach in a Government primary school. I teach Maths and English to grades 3 and 4. I think I am quite a good teacher because I have not only qualification but I have also done the teaching course. I never wanted to become a teacher though, I wanted to become a writer but somehow it did not happen. *(When asked why it did not happen)* To be honest, I don't know why I never became a writer. I am also the **eldest child** of my parents so responsibilities came as early from my school life. I had to help my mother in the kitchen, my younger siblings with their homework and had to do my own studies also. I never got time to pursue writing seriously and also because my **father did not like the idea**.'

2. 'It is very frustrating to work in a Government school. I know I will never get promoted, no matter how hard I work. The school has no funds; my salary is never going to increase. But still it is better than nothing; at least I get to see my **colleagues and friends** everyday. I like children and in my school all teachers are female. **Female are always better with handling children and in a way it is good that they get practise for future life after marriage.**'

3. 'To be honest, it doesn't make a lot of difference whether I work or I do not work, even economically. Half of my salary is spent in the means of transportation to and from school everyday, rest is literally nothing. I keep half of it as pocket money and even from that my younger sisters and brothers take their shares. The other half has to be given to my mother so that she keeps collecting stuff for my **marriage** but that she would do even if I did not work. I don't contribute in the house expenditures.

4. 'Decision making is mostly done by my **father alone** except for one or two occasions where he also consults my mother. I have never been involved even in decisions that we have to take collectively as a family.'

5. 'I don't feel empowered at all. I don't like what I do. I would have felt empowered if I was **at least allowed** if not encouraged to do what I wanted to do with my life. I don't enjoy teaching as much as I would have enjoyed writing. I think because I was not allowed to do what I wanted to, I don't enjoy anything. My father is a very serious minded and **short tempered** person. I once shared with him that I wanted to become a writer but he not only discouraged me but **forced** me to complete bachelors and start teaching in this nearby Government school. Maybe he thinks that it is enough of a career for me.'

Researcher's Observations
The respondent was a very confident, educated and good looking lady from a relatively better off economic background. She spoke against her father fearlessly which was quit a surprise considering the environment around.

Respondent no 3

Profile:

Name: Safia Bibi

Age: 33

Marital Status: Widow with 3 children

Occupation/Nature of work: Domestic maid/Informal economy

Household Structure: Female headed household

Excerpts from semi-structured interview

1. 'I don't know what to say, really. There is nothing much to say about myself.'

2. 'I have been working since I was a **child**. My mother was also a maid, she used to wash clothes in somebody's house and I would always accompany her. When I was fourteen, she started calling me her helper. From that time onwards, I kept working in numerous houses in multiple locations; I had to walk the longest distances in summer and in rain. Three years ago, my husband passed away and then I started looking for a single workplace where I could also take my children. Since then I work as a maid in the house of a very rich family. They have two other servants as well.'

3. 'My salary is spent on the rent of this house, food items and other household essentials. I decide about it though I often listen to my **eldest son**. He is growing up and often insists that I should give him some cash and I do give him, mostly.'

4. 'I take the decisions of our family myself, of course with the consent of my children especially my **eldest son**.'

5. 'I think the life of poor is to serve the rich. This is all by design of destiny but poverty is very bad. How can one ever feel empowered if your own children are not getting to eat what you cook for somebody else's children? This is a very difficult thing to live with on a daily basis. Still I don't question anything but I just need **respect for myself.** I am poor but I want to earn money **through labour and not through humiliation**. I feel very bad if my employers scream at me. Even if I do something wrong, why can't I be corrected politely. I can tell you that **poor people only fall for respect.** But this job is my compulsion as I need to earn to be able to bring up my three children.'

Researcher's Observations

Initially this woman was reluctant to talk but then she herself volunteered. She seemed tired and hurt due to her employers' treatment of her. Also the influence of her son was apparent in her home because her daughters younger to the son were making tea for him.

Respondent no 4

Profile:

Name: Fahmeeda Khatoon

Age: 50 years

Occupation/Nature of work: Banker/Formal economy

Marital Status: Married with two children

Household structure: Nuclear

Excerpts from semi-structured interview

1. 'I am the first woman of my family who has stepped out of the **four walls of the house.** I have been in Bank service for the last fifteen years. There was a lot of opposition that I faced when I first decided to work. Initially my **husband** was also reluctant but I managed to convince him and since then he has largely been supportive. My **eldest brother** was most angry with me and my husband at this decision. He even stopped talking to me for several years but now I am old with grown up children. Support of brothers or parental family becomes irrelevant after marriage, though he is not angry any more. After the marriage, it is the husband who has to be at your side **otherwise life can get very tough.**'

2. 'My work has now become a routine, a part of my life style. It is a bank job and since I am in customer service, I have to engage in a lot of public dealing. My job requires interaction with all kinds of men and sometimes **I don't quite like the looks they give me. When I was young, I was pretty but now with age I feel more secure and capable of insulting anyone one who passes a remark or tries to touch me while**

handing over the cheque or cash. Banking is my profession and I am there just doing my job, it has to be taken seriously and respectfully.'

3. 'I can spend my salary wherever I want to; I think this is quite an exception considering that most of my female colleagues have to give a large share of their salaries to their husbands.'

4. 'As far as the decision making in our family is concerned, it really depends upon the decision. I take the **day to day, simple routine like decisions** but long term **strategic decisions relating to sale or purchase of property or family assets or house construction or children's future are my husband's domain.** In most of the decisions, he consults me but **final word is his**. I don't complain about it because eventually he is the man and the **leader of the family**.'

5. 'I do consider myself empowered because my husband is supportive I think I have spent a major part of my life justifying my career choice to my relatives. I think **women are at a disadvantage in every way**. They are not allowed to do anything they want; somehow the whole family has to get involved when a woman makes a choice. No man in my family ever had to explain anything he chose to do, but I was opposed by everyone. Why do women have to be held accountable for **little and very personal things** they do. If women have to empowered, **only men** can give them that by understanding and respecting them.'

Researcher's Observations

This was the most educated respondent. She was a Masters degree holder, was very analytical about her own experiences and found the interview a good opportunity to reflect and learn from her own experiences.

Respondent no 5

Profile:

Name: Laibah Khan

Age: 20 years

Occupation/Nature of work: Worker in Beauty Saloon/Formal economy

Marital Status: Single

Household Structure: Female headed household

Excerpts from semi-structured interview

1. 'I was very young when my father passed away so me along with all my siblings dropped out of school. My mother did not have enough money to educate us. I don't feel bad about not going to school, **the girls of my age who all went to school then, now stay home and work all day**. What difference does going to school make? Eventually it is the **stove and utensils with which we girls have to work**.'

2. 'I have recently started working, I think it has not been a year as yet. I do it just to earn some money; **no amount is less if you are poor**. I have to do all the **household work** before coming to the saloon. I am the first one to wake up and the last one to go to bed. My mother is sick and can't work anymore and **my brothers cannot help me, they are boys and boys don't do the household work**. But I have now befriended with other girls of my age in the saloon so sometimes we get to **eat and laugh together**. Though mostly there are a lot of customers and our supervisor is around. We avoid even speaking to each other because if the supervisor thinks you are not focused on work, she can deduct a lot of money from your wage.'

3. 'Well, I have to hand all my wages to my mother. She has to get food and clothes for us and so does my brother. We are happy with that. I just wish that I get to spend more time with my friends rather than working from morning till night. I also get new clothes on the occasion of Eid but I think God has a very unfair distribution system though one has to accept destiny.'

4. 'I don't know who takes the decisions. Actually there are no serious decisions except for what to cook etc and my mother takes them.'

5. 'I think **money and peace of mind** are very important, I don't have either so how can there be a feeling of empowerment? Currently I want to attend my childhood friend's wedding in Lahore (another city). Though I don't think I will be able to go, it is far away and the cost of transportation is very high. If I manage to go, I will also need clothes also. All this can cost my two months salary but even then I don't mind. But I know that even I manage to convince my mother, **my brothers will never let me go. They think it is not appropriate for a single young girl to go to another city to attend a function**. Sometimes I don't even understand how come they allowed me to join the saloon, had it not been for the money which I earn, they would have never allowed me.'

Researcher's Observations:

This respondent seemed physically very weak and initially uninterested. The researcher had to engage in a lot of general conversation before getting her to the interviewed. However by the end of the session, she had become very friendly and insisted the researcher to visit her home for lunch.

3.5. Data Analysis

3.5.1. Key Argument

In light of the literature review, conceptual framework and the data presented above, I would like to <u>answer my research question</u> as:

In views and experiences of women at grassroots levels, economic participation by itself does NOT lead to women empowerment

3.5.2. Main Findings

1. Only one of the respondents considered herself empowered and that too was due to the support of her husband. Due to the rigorous gender conditioning women have been subjected to, they hold an inferior view of themselves and a superior view of the men
2. The study reveals a highly unequal status between men and women as women despite being engaged in economic activities were not allowed to make free choices
3. All of them had accepted and scummed to the gendered division of labour and considered household work as the sole responsibility of women.
4. They were underpinning gendered constructs of masculinities and feminities such as men were considered as better strategic decision makers and women were considered better at delicate thread work and in child handling as primary school teachers.
5. Decision making was the domain of men and did not get influenced by women's contribution in the household income at all. Due to the underlying gender inequalities and in equities women do not have a say in decisions effecting their lives.
6. It is hard to say that female headed households were better off. Even where women where the heads of their families, the influence of the sons was obvious due to the patriarchal and male dominated ideology of family life

7. Early marriages and frequent childbirths were among the input factors into the dis-empowered status of women. Savings for dowry and marrying off their daughters also exerted economic and social pressures on women
8. Poverty was a critical factor in the dis-advantaged status of women and it is the girl child who shares the burden of poverty with her mother.
9. Other than the feminization of poverty, it was the in equal power relations between men and women which keep women at a dis-advantaged and un-empowered status
10. Empowerment has different meanings at the individual level. Some of the women wanted a good future for their children, some hinted at respect and dignity for their work and one at money and peace of mind
11. There was a realization that economic activity provides women a platform to form networks and alliance amongst themselves, it allowed them some social space
12. With age, women tend to become secure about their bodies and feel to be in a position to protect themselves
13. The work load on women has doubled as a result of their economic activities outside the household. Household chores remain strictly the unsaid undocumented sole responsibility of women which also gets translated into a gendered division of labour in their children
14. Women's economic participation has been effected a broad range of factors including age, education, marital status, fertility, household structure, intra-household divisions of labour and power
15. Empowerment has a bodily and age sensitive articulation among women. Different stages of life cycle reflected different phases of being empowered or powerless

CHAPTER 4: CONCLUSION

This dissertation reports on a research project that attempted to understand whether market-based approaches to women's empowerment is in keeping with women's own views and experiences. It linked the experiences, views and perspective of women with a review of the literature to try to arrive at a first hand understanding of women's empowerment and economic participation. The first chapter set out the rationale for this research along with defining it's contextual scope and methodology. Chapter 2 synthesized and analyzed the key academic debates and policy approaches towards achieving women's empowerment and economic uplift. As the spirit of the research was to arrive at a conceptual understanding of empowerment from the perspective of women, a conceptual framework was constructed to deconstruct empowerment on the basis of four determinants of empowerment. On the basis of these determinants of empowerment, the qualitative data presented in Chapter 4 was analyzed to answer the research question and arrive at some of the key findings.

My key conclusion is that economic participation alone does not lead to women's empowerment. Access to labour market does not improve the status of women within the household hierarchy and does not influence the power relations in their favour. As discussed earlier, empowerment is a highly relative and complex concept which has different articulations for different individuals, though it is not possible to tackle with empowerment at an individual level. Empowerment is a state of mind which has to come from within and cannot be granted by any outside actor. What the outside actor like Government, NGOs and Donors can do is to create a conducive women friendly environment which enables them to exercise their fee will and choices in life. Providing women with a social space free of discrimination, violence and fear is the first step. Women's empowerment is a process that challenges and transforms the patriarchal beliefs and institutions that reinforce and perpetuate women's inequality (Kabeer: 2001). As a starting point, the Government of Pakistan should take measures to make work places safe and secure for women. It should give exemplary punishment to perpetuators of physical, sexual and verbal harassment of women at their work and in public places.

Empowerment is about making choices with free will. As one respondent said 'I would have felt empowered if I was allowed if not encouraged to do what I wanted to do with my life.' But women's economic participation by itself does not improve the lives and experiences of women. It has to be recognized at the policy level that gender based interventions are socially transformative and unless the underlying gender inequalities, inequities and constructs of masculinity and feminity are not addressed, the status of women within the household and in society at large will not improve. There is a need for equity and equality between the roles, responsibilities, powers and rewards distributed between men and women. This will require a long term process of social change and cultural transformation particularly in the Pakistani society, which is predominantly patriarchal. Globalization can potentially be the most important catalyst for this change and should be capitalized upon as an opportunity for mass education, rural-urban and international migration, technological advancements and access to information and socio-cultural exchange of goods, services, capital and people across the world.

Gender research and analysis has to be at the heart of all Government's policy making and planning. Women have to be at the centre of poverty alleviation and sustainable livelihoods strategies because it is the feminization of poverty which keeps women vulnerable to dis-empowerment and dis advantage. Women poverty reduction and empowerment have to be tackled simultaneously with a two-fold strategy. Donors and NGOs should make more resources available for improving the living conditions of women. Direct Budgetary Support

(DBS) should be provided to women living in extreme poverty to pull them out and Conditional Cash Transfers (CCT) to help them establish a foot hold in society through entrepreneurship, micro-enterprise development and small scale industry. Women's economic and social well-being go hand in hand and cannot be isolated with each other. Women's economic, political and social empowerment has to go together.

Moral support should be provided to women by NGOs, civil society organizations and media through increasing awareness among both women and men about women's rights to have full control over their body, sexuality, fertility and political or religious affiliation. The NGOs should reach out to women at the grass root levels and educate them in an effective manner about their equality of status and rights vis-à-vis men. Communities should be targeted by involving the more influential stakeholders like religious leaders or local politicians in the process. Media should portray a positive and equal role of women and men to challenge and gradually change the unequal gendered constructs and socio-cultural practices.

The misuse of the concept 'women's empowerment' needs to be recognized and rectified. It is conveniently used as a fuzzy jargon, by a host of development organizations and NGOs. Women's empowerment has to be understood in a broader social policy agenda which mobilizes agency to bring about a socio-cultural transformation. I also think that a lot of meaningful research and theoretical perspectives about women's empowerment exist but fall short of being translated into concrete policy decisions and then their on ground implementation. Women empowerment has to be achieved in an overall conducive policy environment, within an effective framework of institutional governance which addresses the roles and responsibilities of different players including the government, donors, NGOs, civil society and communities. Not to mention political commitment and an adequately capacitated resource base which go a long way in realizing gender and development outcomes in a definitive manner.

REFERENCES

Journals

Ali, K (2000) 'Structural Adjustment Policies and Women in the Labour Market: Urban Working Women in Pakistan' *Third World Planning Review* **22** (1): 1-21.

Bridget, A (2001) 'Just Another Job? Paying for Domestic Work' *Gender and Development* **9** (1): 25-33.

Beteta, H. C (2006) 'What is missing in measures of women's empowerment?' *Journal of Human Development and Capabilities* **7** (2): 221-241.

Brenda, B (2008) 'Women entrepreneurs in Nepal: what prevents them from leading the sector?' *Gender and Development* **16** (3): 549-564.

Cerrutti, M (2000) 'Economic Reform, Structural Adjustment and Female Labour Participation in Buenos Aires, Argentina' *World Development* **28** (5): 879-51.

Charmes, J. and Wieringa, S. (2003) 'Measuring Women's Empowerment: an assessment of the Gender related Development Index and Gender Empowerment Measure' *Journal of Human Development and Capabilities* **4** (3): 419-435

Chant, S (2003) Female household Headship and the feminization of poverty: Facts, Fictions and Forward strategies. LSE Gender Institute New working paper Series. Issue 9.

Eyben, R. and Moore, R.N. (2009) 'Choosing words with care? Shifting meanings of women's empowerment in international development' *Third World Quarterly* **30** (2): 285-300.

Esping-Andersen, G. (2007) 'More Inequality and Fewer Opportunities? Structural Determinants and Human Agency in the Dynamics of Income Distribution' *Global Inequality*, London: Polity, pp 216-251

Folbre, N (2006) 'Measuring Care: Gender, Empowerment and the Care Economy' *Journal of Human Development and Capabilities* **7** (2): 183-199.

Faulkner, A. and Lawson, V. (1991) 'Employment versus Empowerment A Case Study of Women's Work in Ecuador' *Journal of Development Studies* **27** (4): 16-47.

Grown, C. and Sebstad, J (1989) 'Introduction: Towards a Wider Perspective on Women's Employment' *World Development* **17** (7): 937-52.

Hunt, J and Kasynathan, N (2001) 'Pathways to Empowerment? Reflections on Microfinance and Transformation in Gender Relations in South Asia' *Gender and Development* **9** (1): 42-52

Hancock, P (2001) 'Rural Women earning Income in Indonesian Factories: The Impact on Gender Relations' *Gender and Development* **9** (1): 18-24.

Horgan, G (2001) 'How does globalization affect women'. International Socialism Journal. Issue 92.

Kabeer, N (1999) 'Resources, Agency, Achievements: Reflections on the Measurement of Women's Empowerment' *Development and Change* **30** (3): 435-64.

Moser, C and Moser, A (2005) 'Gender Mainstreaming Since Beijing: A Review of Success and Limitations in International Institutions', *Gender and Development* **13** (2): 11-22.

Seguino, S. (2000) 'Gender inequality and economic growth: A cross-country analysis' *World Development* **28** (7):1211-1230.

Staveren, I (2001) 'Gender bias in Finance Author(s)' *Gender and Development* **9** (1): 9-17.

Taborga, C. (2009) 'Women's economic empowerment: realities and challenges for the future' *International Social Science Journal* **59** (191): 27-34.

Books

Afshar, H and Dennis, C (1992) Women and Adjustment Policies in the Third World Macmillan:Houndmills

Bhagwati, J. (2004) *In Defence of Globalisation*, Oxford: Oxford University Press

Kabeer, N. (2008) "Chapter 2, Gender and Trends in the Global Force: New and Persisting Forms of Vonerability" *Mainstreaming Gender in Social Protection for the Informal Economy.* pp.27-53, London: Commonwealth Secretariat

Milanovic, B. (2005) *Worlds Apart*, Princeton and Oxford: Princeton University Press

Stichter, S. (1990) *Women, employment and family in the international division of labour*: Macmillan Press Limited.

Tsing, A. (2005) *Friction: An Ethnography of Global Connection*, Princeton and Oxford: Priceton University Press

Reports

Government of Pakistan (1973) *Constitution of Islamic Republic of Pakistan*

Goetz, A. M. and R. S. Gupta (1996) *Who Takes the Credit? Gender, Power, and Control over Loan Use in Rural Credit Programmes in Bangladesh'*: Institute of Development Studies, University of Sussex, Brighton, UK.

International Labour Office (ILO) (2006) *Gender Equality and Decent Work: Good Practices at the Workplace* Geneva: International Labour Office

Ministry of Education Government of Pakistan (2007) *Education in Pakistan-A White Paper*

Population Division, Department of Economic and Social Affairs, United Nations Secretariat, (2001) *Workshop on Prospects of Fertility decline in High Fertility Countries*

UNDP (2005) *Human Development Report 2005*, International cooperation at a crossroads. Aid, trade and security in an unequal world

UNRISD (2005) *Report on Gender Equality: Striving for Justice in an Unequal World*

VDM publishing house ltd.

Scientific Publishing House

offers

free of charge publication

of current academic research papers, Bachelor´s Theses, Master's Theses, Dissertations or Scientific Monographs

If you have written a thesis which satisfies high content as well as formal demands, and you are interested in a remunerated publication of your work, please send an e-mail with some initial information about yourself and your work to *info@vdm-publishing-house.com*.

Our editorial office will get in touch with you shortly.

VDM Publishing House Ltd.
Meldrum Court 17.
Beau Bassin
Mauritius
www.vdm-publishing-house.com

LaVergne, TN USA
05 December 2010

207429LV00004B/243/P